Tomorrow
I have to get an
MRI

London and Faythe Daniels

BARNSLEY INK
RALEIGH, NORTH CAROLINA

Tomorrow I Have To get an MRI
Copyright © 2024 Faythe Daniels and London Daniels

Printed in the United States of America
ISBN 978-1-956543-52-0

Book layout by CSinclaire Write-Design LLC
Illustrations by Ayyan Designs

• BARNSLEY INK •
RALEIGH, NORTH CAROLINA

London Daniels is a 10-year-old girl diagnosed with Neurofibromatosis Type 1 (NF1). This is a genetic disorder that causes tumors to grow along the nerves.

As a part of monitoring NF1, London has to get an MRI every three months. (She may be an expert on this process!)

This can be scary for someone who is experiencing an MRI for the first time, so she wanted to help prepare kids when they need to say . . .

"Tomorrow I have to get an MRI."

Hi, my name is London, and I'm 10 years old. Today I'm going to teach you about getting an MRI.

An MRI is a scan that doctors use to look inside your body or head. I've had several.

Guess what?!
You will probably miss a day of school.

Who wouldn't want a day off
from school?

When I check in, I give them
my name and date of birth.

They give me a wrist band with
my information on it.

You are not alone!

An adult may be able to go
in the room with you. My mom and dad
like to come in with me.

After you arrive, a nurse will
take you to a locker room.

You have to take off your shoes and
change into a gown and socks.

The nurses check your temperature and your blood pressure.

Don't worry, taking your blood pressure doesn't hurt. It's just a little squeeze on your arm.

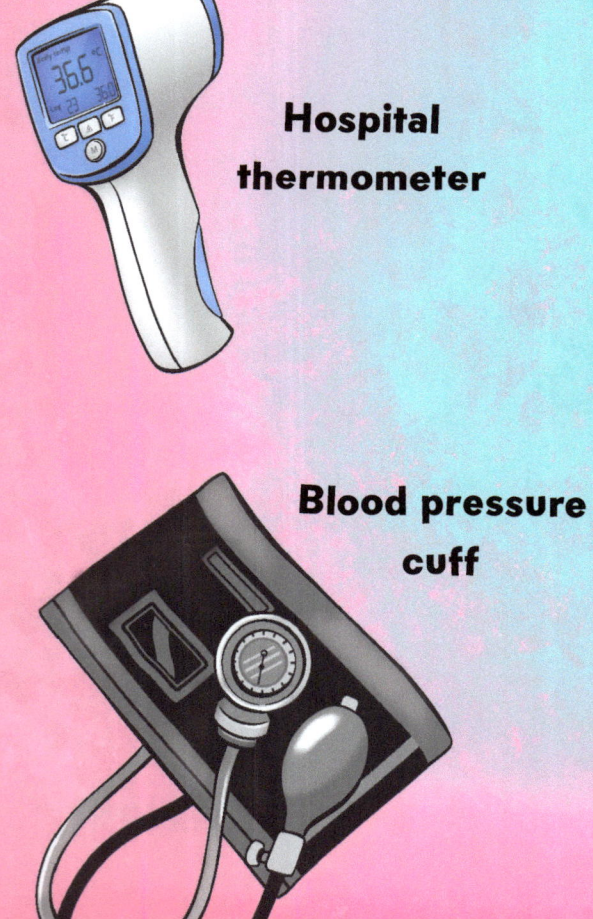

Hospital thermometer

Blood pressure cuff

A nurse may need to insert an IV in your arm. It will hurt a little (sort of like a pinch and a shot at the same time), but I close my eyes, take a deep breath, and squeeze my mom's hand.

Before you go in the MRI,
you need to be scanned
with a metal detector wand.
I have to walk through a scanner too.
They like to double-check!
This does not hurt at all.

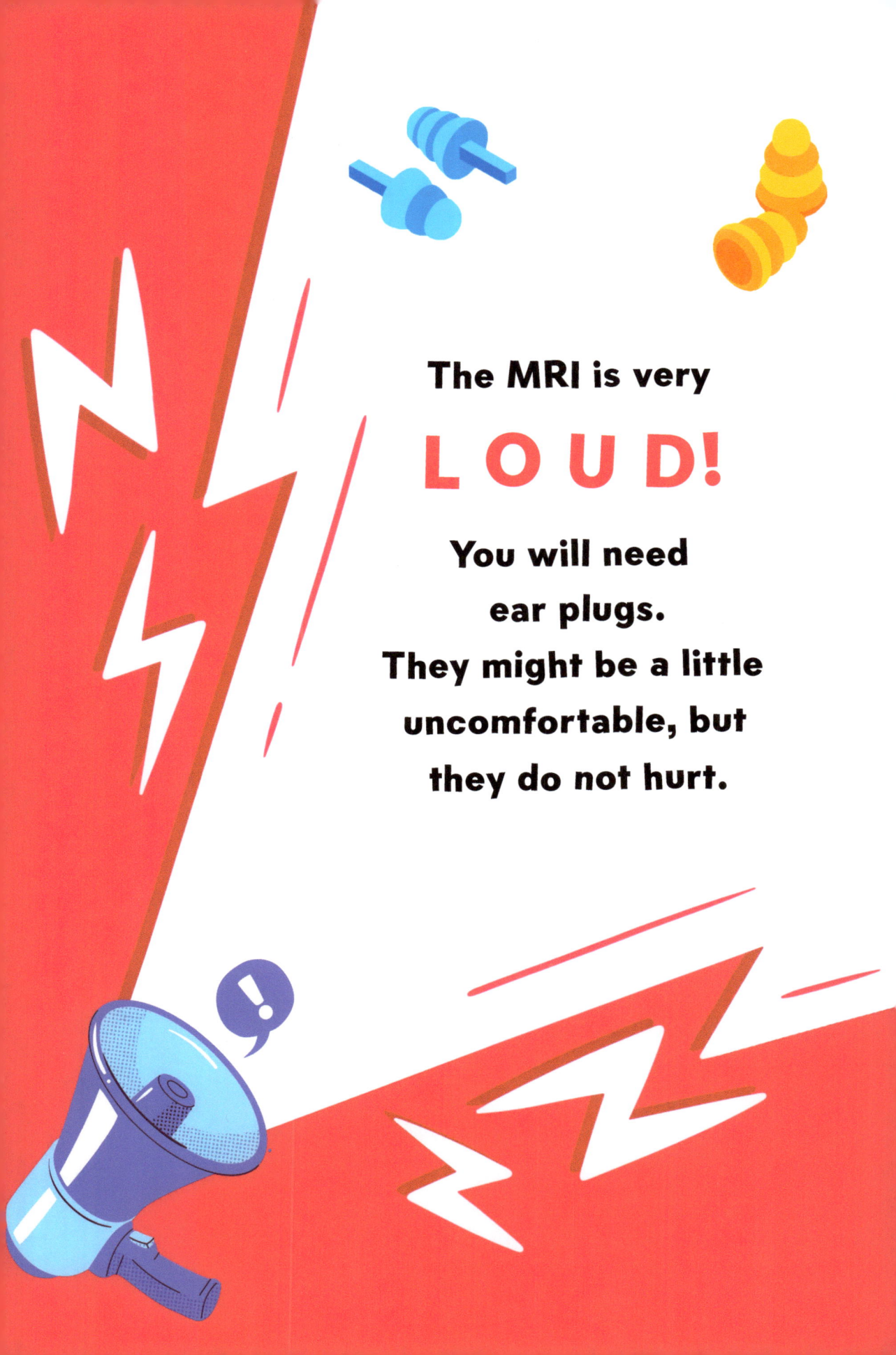

The MRI is very

LOUD!

You will need
ear plugs.
They might be a little
uncomfortable, but
they do not hurt.

Sometimes you might get headphones to listen to music during the MRI.

Sometimes they have cool goggles to watch your favorite movie or show! Don't worry, they give you headphones so you can hear!

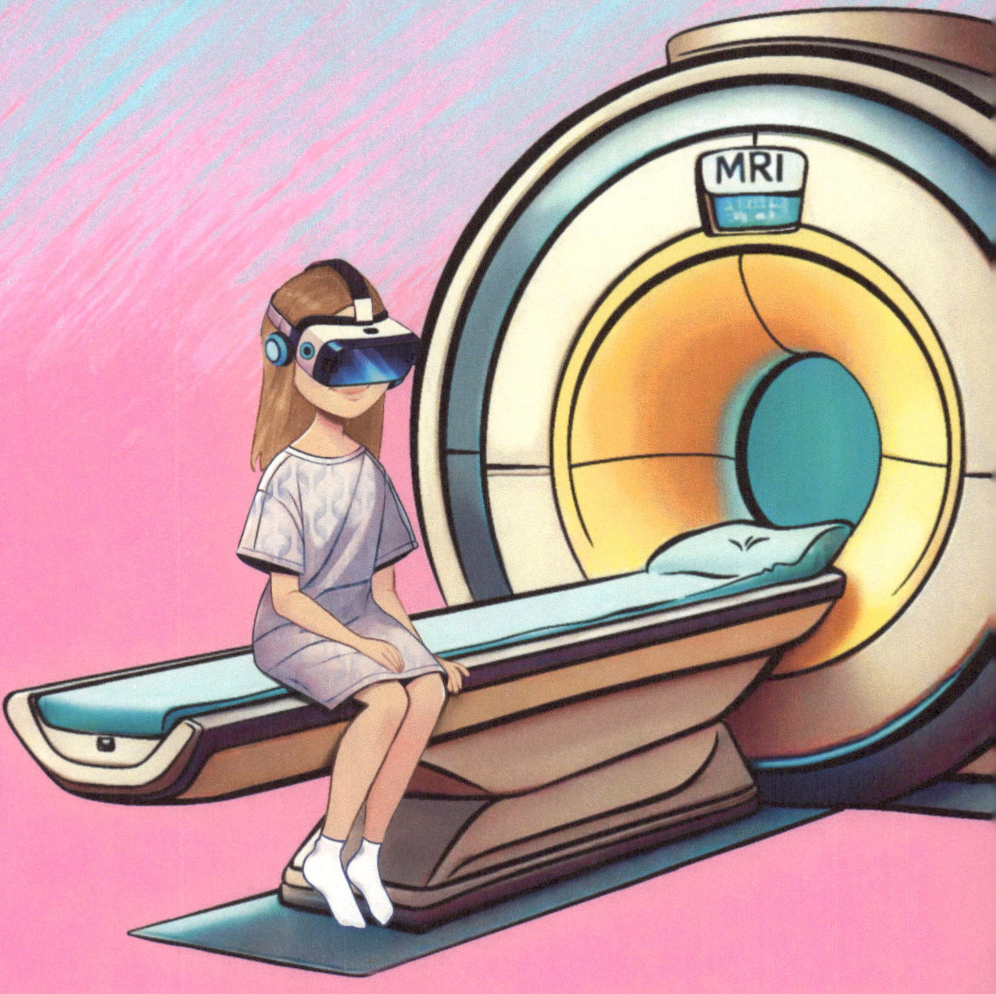

Sometimes I fall asleep.
That's okay.
You might fall asleep too!

ALMOST TIME TO GO IN!

While you are lying on the MRI bed, you can have a blanket to keep you warm and a pillow for your head!

When you are going into the MRI,
it may look like you won't fit
because there's not much room.

But you will fit!

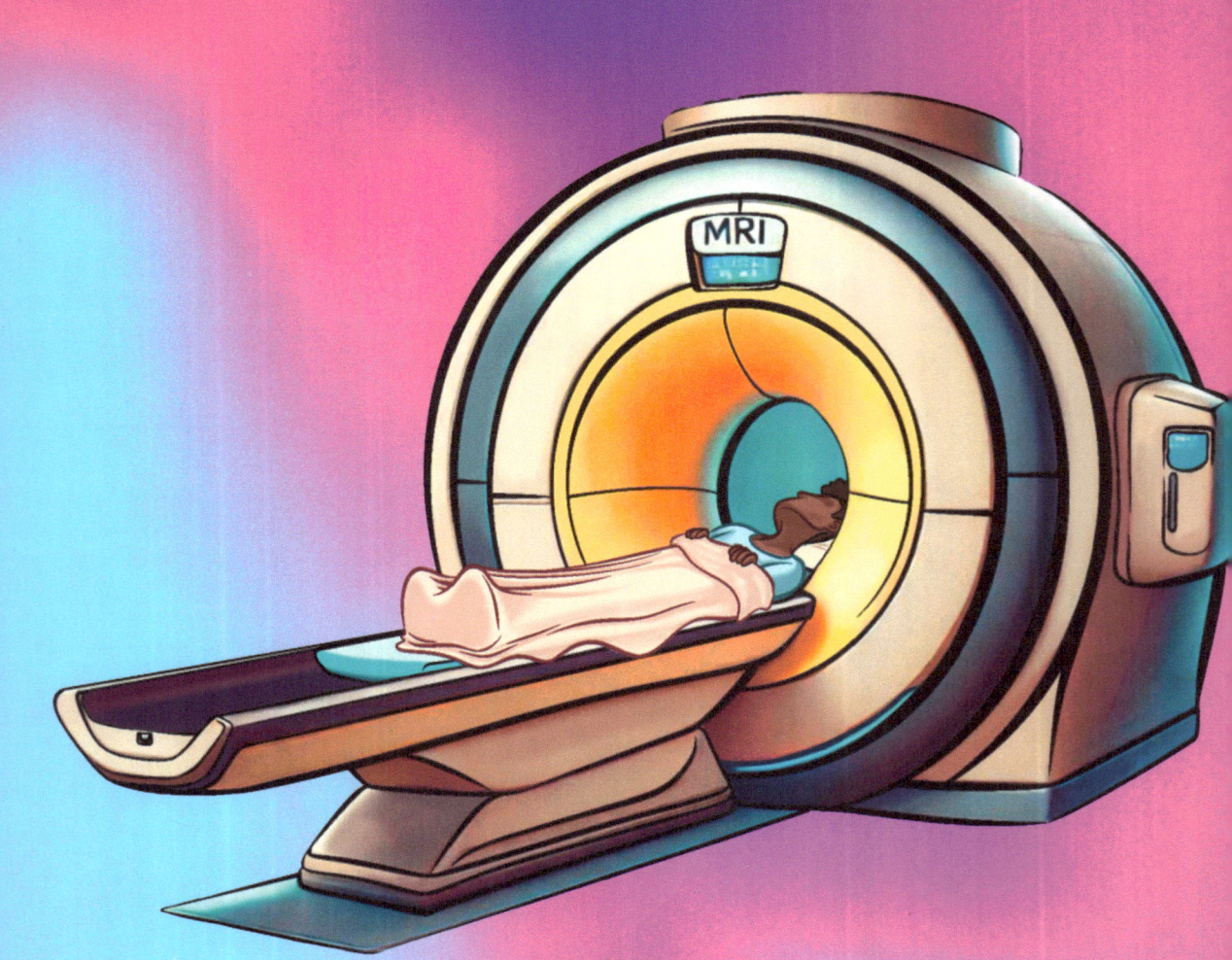

You need to lie very still
while you are in the MRI.

If you move, the doctor may
have to take extra pictures,
and no one wants that.

NO MOVEMENT

After a few pictures,
the nurse will come in and set up
the bag of liquid contrast to go into
the IV in your arm.

The contrast may give you a cold
feeling. The cold feeling goes away
after the testing is over.

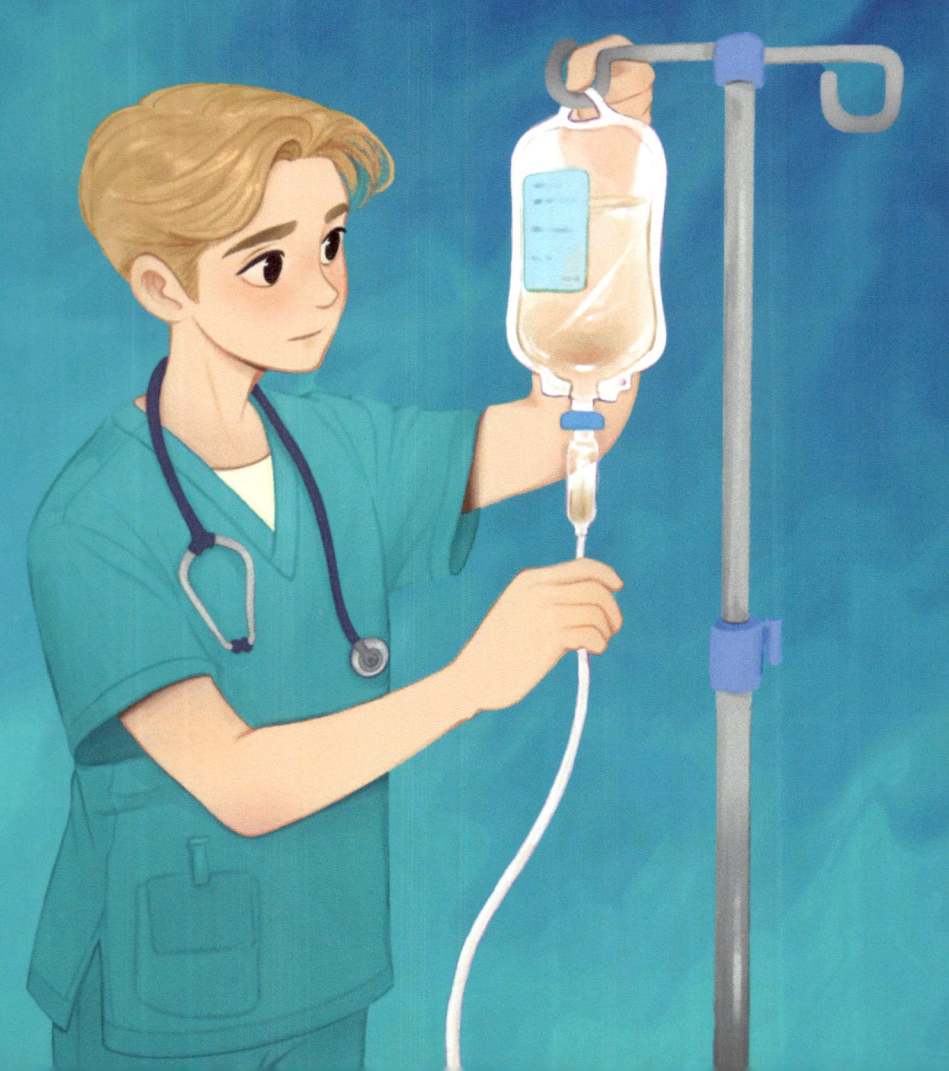

There is an
MRI technician
looking at the pictures
while you are in the
machine. There is
also a nurse to keep
an eye on you.

The MRI can take about one hour.

Before you know it,

you are . . .

ALL DONE!

**Sometimes the nurses
let you choose a prize, because
getting an MRI is not easy!**

A radiologist will review your pictures and report back to your caregiver.

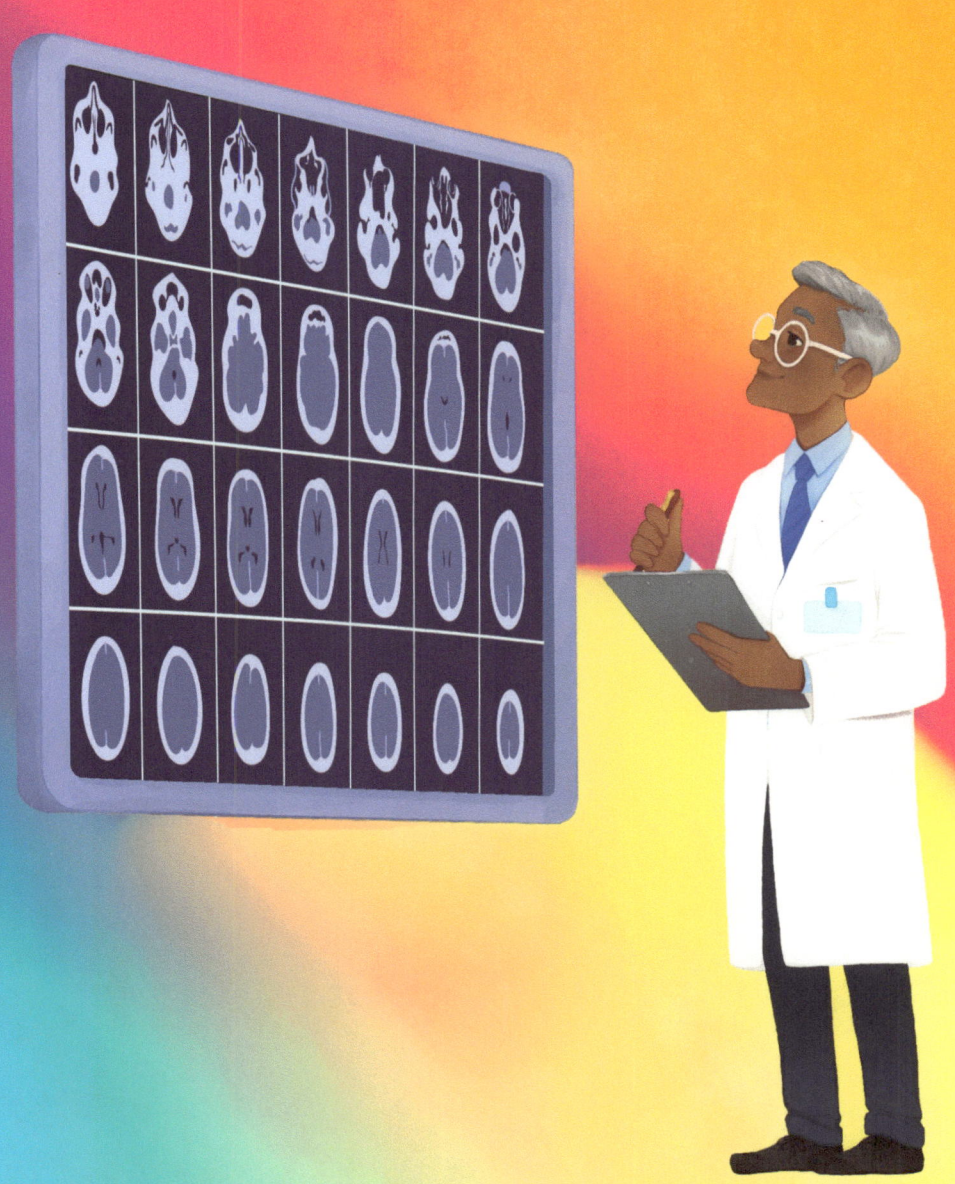

I know getting
an MRI may be
a little scary.

But I hope I helped
make it easier by
letting you know
what to expect!

Just remember . . .

WORD DEFINITIONS!

MRI (Magnetic Resonance Imaging): A machine that produces magnetic and radio waves to create images

Contrast: A dye that highlights organs, vessels, and tissue in your body

Radiologist: A doctor who uses imaging to help treat people

IV (Intravenous Line): A soft, flexible tube placed inside a vein

www.ingramcontent.com/pod-product-compliance
Lightning Source LLC
Chambersburg PA
CBHW041447120626
46547CB00002B/376